Stages of New Longings

- Madysson Yezh

Stages of New Longings

Madysson Yezh

Madysson Yezh

"Growing emotions" are tough to deal with,

but...

what's in life without 'em?

Dedicated to,

future Maddy.

Stages of New Longings

CONTENTS

Stages of New Longings

Preface

Hi! I'm Madysson Yezh, a teen with an interest in a plethora of distinct fields. I've never been able to stick to one field of interest for a long time, but somehow, writing has stuck around for quite a while. This is my first book, and I hope I can produce more in the future.

To be completely honest, the book is more of a keepsake I want to have for myself, but at the same time, I'm happy to share my little point of view on everything around me with the world.

Growing up intensifies all the hormones, and if that isn't enough, there are people around you telling you what to do or not to do. I'm not blaming them, but this is the part of life where you want to experience things. I'd encourage experiencing things rather than living off others' life experiences (that's boring).

Note: The poems are totally based on my own experiences, and there might be some words or experiences to which one might not relate. I totally get it, but please don't come back at me if you feel like there's too much immorality expressed by a common teen. I can assure you that most of us go through these and more varied scenarios. Of course, we aren't as old as many, but that doesn't diminish the way we feel or view the world. We might go through similar plots that one might face in adulthood—after all, we're being prepped for the near future.

Madysson Yezh.

:D

Stages of New Longings

Madysson Yezh

Blue Aesthetics.

How blue you look,
Like the glossy sea.
On a clear place,
Is where you'll be.

The Birds go with you,
The airplanes too.
Just so much beauty,
Hidden within you.

The days I've spent,
Tracking the moon,
On you being your best!

The glossy nights,
I've seen you as.
But there will come a day,
Where I'm a part of you.

Stages of New Longings

Written on & at:
19/05/2022,
15:44.

<u>Thoughts.</u>

Madysson Yezh

Stages of New Longings

Dark Nostalgia.

The darkest nights,
The loneliest phases,
Those sad pasts,
All to be forgotten.

Laughter looking back at cries,
But memories though the glimpses of the
past.

Dark tears rolling down,
But the mist from the past,
Never seems to leave.

Going through the vintage aesthetics,
Strolling down those rainy sights,
In my favorite bridge of sighs.

The nostalgia felt so hard,
Reverting back those old days.
Unexplainable and perplexing life
situations,
That I've somehow overcome.

Stages of New Longings

Still getting through,
Reminiscing about the past,
With petrifying hallucinations.
Living in a nightmare full of glum,
No way to escape but to outlast times.

Madysson Yezh

Written on & at:
Some evening in June, 2022.

<u>Thoughts.</u>

Stages of New Longings

Madysson Yezh

Eternal Nature.

The cold breeze hitting my face,
Then there's me with a drowsy face.
Eternal glory,
Eternal greenery,
All throughout the path.

In the midst of the mists on the mount,
Getting colder and colder,
As we drive up high,
The sun's getting nearer to the sky.

The gold laden sunshine, uprising me.

Then between the woods and the trees,
Small civilizations but happy faces.

Stages of New Longings

Written on & at:
31/06/2022,
20:50.

<u>Thoughts.</u>

Madysson Yezh

Stages of New Longings

Madysson Yezh

The Ice Queen's Perspective.

Running through the veins,
The cold blood of the past heirs.
Thy queen of the realm.

Places so frosted,
Hearts so cold,
Watching by the windows,
Out the castle doors,
The hostile breeze and their vows.

Looking up the ether,
The white sky,
The cold breeze,
Maybe the end and epilogue.

Stages of New Longings

Written on & at:
09/08/2022,
12:50.

<u>Thoughts.</u>

Madysson Yezh

Stages of New Longings

Madysson Yezh

Shimmering Wonder.

Looking at you from afar,
A sudden look to kill any heart.
The beauty,
The smart.

The kind of you never be seen,
nor looked for,
Can't be glared at,
No one, but the lucky her.

You're so full of amazingness,
Your shimmer,
Your dazzle,
Catching eyes, but never sighs.

Stages of New Longings

Written on & at:
07/11/2022,
07:56.

Thoughts.

Madysson Yezh

Stages of New Longings

Madysson Yezh

The Winter Greet.

As I look out the window,
The sun rises.
Looking at the sight of snow,
Makes me glow.

Light shining through the clouds,
It stands up proud,
Through the winter haze.

But will it last long?
We wouldn't know.
But until next summer,
I can't wait to have my best winter.

In a small story of my living,
All my years been filled up with you.
The beauty that resides,
The snow, the fog, the cold.

Nearing the rest,
The rest of breeze,
The rest of freeze.
Until the next awaken;

I Will always be waiting,
For winter's next appearing.

Written on & at:
07/12/2022,
21:15.

Thoughts.

Stages of New Longings

Madysson Yezh

Luminated Moments.

At a dark room,
The power went out.
I see you light,
In the shimmering bright.
Sittin' at the corner of the room,
But, giving the creeps?
Not what you'd do,
Good shimmering light.

Raining outside,
Sitting with a bunch of people,
Sharing the same vibe.
I love this feeling,
Experienced only by me,
No one would ever know,
How it feels.

A different aura,
Surrounding us all,
No good lighting,
But this might last.

Oh dear light,
How good you were.

But even now,
Your presence is where.

Madysson Yezh

Written on & at:
17/01/2023,
08:40.

Thoughts.

Stages of New Longings

Madysson Yezh

Phoenix of the Heart.

Beginnings are tough,
But its light to the heart.
For it has overcome much rust,
And has been left with just the crust.

Lost but never found,
The heart so intricate,
It searches each crook.
Certainly no bound,
That it stops with its nook.

Unstable minds,
Irrelevant buds,
Golden age of laden, of confusion
And new bones arising.
The last one grew some heart bones,
Are you too here to grow more?

For, destiny can only tell,
What will lie beside one.

Will it be you,
That my heart will beat?

Written on & at:
02/09/2024,
20:54

Thoughts.

Stages of New Longings

Madysson Yezh

Everlasting?

Mists in the sky,
you're all in my eye.
Blinding my see,
but bringing me the sea.

Oceans at night,
Glossy seas in sight.
sparkles of water,
one hundred thoughts.
but i just wish
my dim pasts never curl.

Ominous approaches,
makes the day not so pleasant.
But life's never decent,
Without evanescent emotions

Now that its time,
I let my wings fly.
The fire inside me,
burns till it's free.

Stages of New Longings

Written on & at:
09/09/2024,
21:36.

Thoughts.

Madysson Yezh

Stages of New Longings

Madysson Yezh

The Endless Cerulean.

Bound to end,
Does make me tend.
You're so full of joy,
Endless blue sky.

Housing me in,
Like no one has ever.
At noon you're so white,
And at dawn not so bright.

Untold envy,
That I hold upon you.
For your shine make it vanish,
The envy that I bestow.

Varied choices,
I ask myself within.
But could I ever become you?

At some point in my life,
Aged 80 or 90,
will it be my greatest hope,
to be one with you.

Stages of New Longings

Written on & at:
10/09/2024,
13:32.

<u>Thoughts.</u>

Madysson Yezh

Stages of New Longings

Eartha Shrieks.

Her the lotte on your geo,
Keep 'er safe within your azure.
For they've come to fetch thy out,
Dare you not let.

You've become for senile,
Ought not forget river Nile.
For they've come to fetch 'er out,
Dare you not let.

Rampages throughout the map,
They've forgot to wear their caps.
All they've done to tear you apart,
And yet manifested no regard.

Truce sounds to none,
Not for 'er nor to geo.
They've let you extinct.
But you still act host,
To them the parasites.

Stages of New Longings

Written on & at:
14/09/2024,
12:22.

<u>Thoughts.</u>

Madysson Yezh

Stages of New Longings

Madysson Yezh

New World.

New to the world, am I?
This feeling so different.
Is it just me?
Or do all go through?

Ecstasy unchanged,
But looking at the 'ness,
Makes me return.

Soft ripples in the water,
But at your presence, notice, will I?
Much doubted,
For your stars are magnetic.

Hurt me will you never,
But when you do so,
Heart so porous,
Let 'er be, please.

Stages of New Longings

Written on & at:
27/09/2024,
03:10.

<u>Thoughts.</u>

47

Stages of New Longings

Madysson Yezh

Sowed and Seeped.

There once was a small little star,
She waved her arms, no scar.
Living the life one could wish,
Living like it's a dream
That has no end.

Out, comes the endless sky,
rolling down
Embracing her,
with its evil red carpet.

Unbeknownst to the star,
She walks down the path,
With faith and glory.

Grunting and cries,
Whispering and pries.
She showered down the rain,
For whatever-so the pain.

Hunters then came,
Her glory went in vain,
The pain in her veins,
Show the sky with a crane.

Written on & at:
29/10/2024,
19:09.

Thoughts.

Stages of New Longings

Tis Thy.

Mine are you?
For when I laid my eyes,
I saw you true,
Loads that pry.

Yours am I?
For you've annihilated my heart.
The rose was burnt much
thy flame that's wurt.

Lucid are, my wants dear cupid
Being cutched up with you, that's vivid.
Oneiric imaginations that I have,
They didn't come in a day or two.

Original's thy care,
venomous my stare.
The look that you give,
that makes me still.

Stages of New Longings

Vicious it is your smile,
Your so insecure laughter.
For I want to smother you with joy,
and lure you with my coy.

Ethereal it is,
In our passion, we are whiz
Take me in,
cover me with your beauty,
engulf me uncut.

Written on & at:
20/01/2025,
23:44.

Thoughts.

Stages of New Longings

Madysson Yezh

For Thy.

The calendar so withered,
Life feels tethered,
For it's been so lathered,
That nothing else mattered.

Souls now owned,
The buzz still droned.
Heads were crowned,
Happy, the towned.

The wound she so carried,
Left her much scurried.
They left, for her be buried,
Yet, she tarried.

Stages of New Longings

Written on & at:
23/01/2025,
23:05.

<u>Thoughts.</u>

Madysson Yezh

Stages of New Longings

Acknowledgments.

Firstly, let me take a moment to appreciate a few people who've stayed with my writing journey and have joined it midway. If not for these critiques, I wouldn't have gotten the guts to publish this book. FJ my absolute bestie, you've been here since the start, reading the writings and you're the only one who knows the reason behind each poem <3, and helped me through when I had second thoughts of publishing this. MH, KAV, CS, AA, SV, and AR… my beta-readers!
These guys have never given up on me at any point in time, and even though most of the poems were cringe, they've gritted their teeth and stayed with me the whole time.

To my parents and my broo, it was just an idea to publish this book, without y'all's support, I wouldn't have published this <3.

To everyone who's reading the book by your own interest or because I forced you to, thank you so much for purchasing my book and giving it a read <3.

Thanking all the ones that have made me draft the poem in the first place, once again. Love y'all tons!